JENNY CARR KINNEY

Quilting Designs from the Past

300+ Designs from 1810–1940

Carolyn,
I hope this
helps you answer the
question...
"How do I quilt it?"
Fondly
Jenny Carr Kinney

C&T PUBLISHING

Text copyright © 2008 by Jenny Carr Kinney

Artwork copyright © 2008 by C&T Publishing, Inc.

Publisher: Amy Marson

Creative Director: Gailen Runge

Editor: Stacy Chamness

Technical Editor: Susan Nelsen

Copyeditor: Wordfirm Inc.

Proofreader: Christine Mann

Cover Designer: Kristy K. Zacharias

Book Designer: Rose Sheifer-Wright

Production Coordinator: Zinnia Heinzmann

Illustrators: Tim Manibusan, Kirstie L. Pettersen, and Jason Francis

Photography: Luke Mulks, Diane Pedersen, and Christina Carty-Francis of C&T Publishing unless otherwise noted

Published by C&T Publishing, Inc., P.O. Box 1456, Lafayette, CA 94549

Library of Congress Cataloging-in-Publication Data

Carr Kinney, Jenny
  Quilting designs from the past : 300+ designs from 1810–1940 / Jenny Carr Kinney.
    p. cm.
  Includes bibliographical references.
  Summary: "Quilting Designs from the Past features more than 300 traditional quilting designs popular through time periods from 1810 to 1940"--Provided by publisher.
  ISBN 978-1-57120-534-6 (paper trade : alk. paper)
  1. Quilting--United States--Patterns. I. Title.

TT835.C376 2008
746.46'041--dc22

                    2008008318

Printed in China
10 9 8 7 6 5 4 3 2 1

Dedication

This book is dedicated to my mother, Carley Jane Canfield Carr, who gave me a gift—the ability to have a passion. Hers was music, mine is quilting. She taught me through example that commitment and enthusiasm can make dreams come true. I know she would be proud of my accomplishments.

Acknowledgments

I have wanted to present the material in this book for a long time. I could not have developed this goal and made steps to realize this dream without the mentoring of my early teachers. Charlotte Ekback shared her passion for antique quilts and taught me to look beyond the colors. Sharon Norbutas inspired me from the beginning and I continue to enjoy her insight and advice on teaching in the classroom and pursuing dreams.

Colleagues, friends, and family whose expertise, background, and experience I value helped make this book a reality. Lynn Kempton, Jeanne Kinney, Pamela Roberts Lindsay, Marsh Peters, and Lori Rees, thank you for your friendship, suggestions, and support.

Some of the designs included in this book come from family quilts owed by Pam Dixon and Lois Lautzenhiser NaDal. Pamela Roberts Lindsay, and Ken and Lori Rees generously offered their quilt collections as additional resources of design.

Additionally, I wish to thank Harriet Hargrave for her help and encouragement, and my husband, Philip Kinney, for his love and understanding (and computer skills).

Contents

Introduction

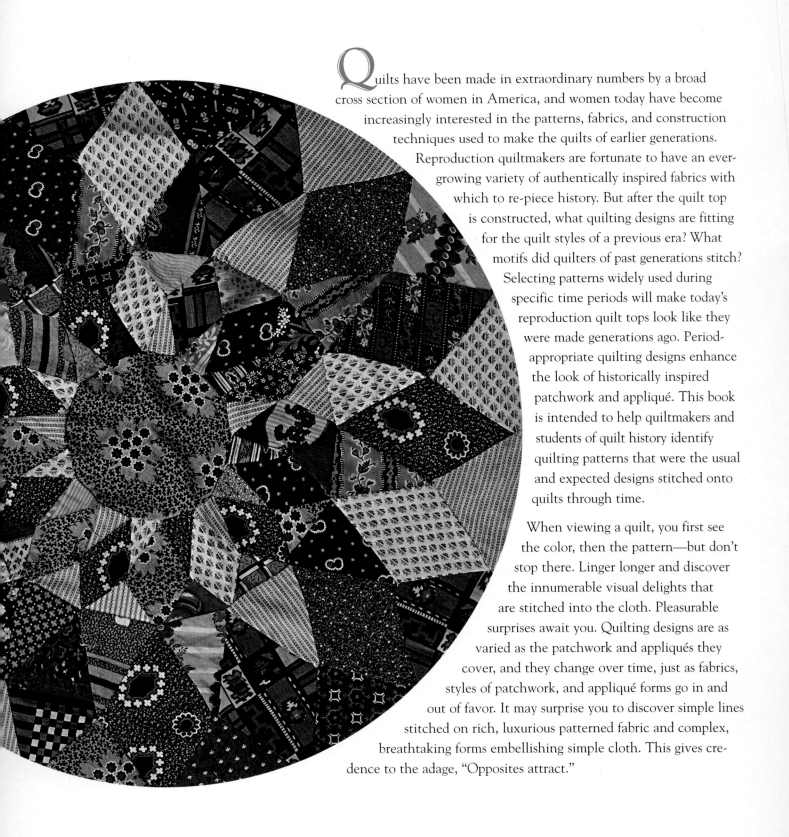

Quilts have been made in extraordinary numbers by a broad cross section of women in America, and women today have become increasingly interested in the patterns, fabrics, and construction techniques used to make the quilts of earlier generations. Reproduction quiltmakers are fortunate to have an ever-growing variety of authentically inspired fabrics with which to re-piece history. But after the quilt top is constructed, what quilting designs are fitting for the quilt styles of a previous era? What motifs did quilters of past generations stitch? Selecting patterns widely used during specific time periods will make today's reproduction quilt tops look like they were made generations ago. Period-appropriate quilting designs enhance the look of historically inspired patchwork and appliqué. This book is intended to help quiltmakers and students of quilt history identify quilting patterns that were the usual and expected designs stitched onto quilts through time.

When viewing a quilt, you first see the color, then the pattern—but don't stop there. Linger longer and discover the innumerable visual delights that are stitched into the cloth. Pleasurable surprises await you. Quilting designs are as varied as the patchwork and appliqués they cover, and they change over time, just as fabrics, styles of patchwork, and appliqué forms go in and out of favor. It may surprise you to discover simple lines stitched on rich, luxurious patterned fabric and complex, breathtaking forms embellishing simple cloth. This gives credence to the adage, "Opposites attract."

*Just like an antique quilt, a well-made reproduction
will never lose its power to charm.*

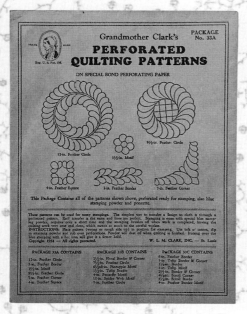

Quilting stitches are primarily structural, holding the layers together and keeping the batting from migrating, but they may be much more decorative, full of elements that create a whole new layer of design. This book presents examples, both simple and complex, of how quilts were quilted during the nineteenth and early twentieth centuries. Books and periodicals that quiltmakers might have read provide inspiration for quilt designs: household help magazines, needlework newspaper articles and books, commercial patterns, and actual quilts from the specific time period under study. Museums and private collections contain examples of extraordinary quilting. I do not address different regional or cultural characteristics here, for it is my intent to illustrate the usual and expected ways quilters in America quilted between 1810 and 1940. I also selected some fancy patterning that is representative of motifs seen during each era.

The quilting treatment of any patchwork or appliqué design has a significant effect on the outcome of the finished piece. Reproducing quilts from another era requires selecting not only suitable patchwork and appliqué patterns and fabrics, but period-appropriate quilting designs as well. Just like an antique quilt, a well-made reproduction will never lose its power to charm.

The quilt pattern choice is, of course, left to the maker, but it is my hope that these pages will inspire you to make quilts from historical inspiration. The pattern ideas in this book can be adapted for any quilt top. Find what was stylish for the period, and, like the quiltmakers of yesteryear, adapt it to fit your skill level. The quilt top is your blank canvas. By all means, use your creative imagination.

This book is intended as a guide for makers of reproduction and traditional quilts, as a reference for students of quilt history, and as a source of information for anyone who appreciates the quilting stitches that cover the quilts of the past.

Relatively few American quilts exist from the first quarter of the nineteenth century. These surviving quilts each have their own unique qualities, but an inspection of the quilting patterns uncovers many similarities. Closely stitched parallel lines, pointed oval leaves, and grids are some of the recurring and expected patterns found stitched into quilts made during this period. These common quilting patterns appear on a number of quilt styles that were popular at this time.

WHOLECLOTH QUILTS

One of the earliest quilt styles is the wholecloth quilt. It is predominantly made of a single fabric. Several panels are sewn together to achieve a desired size. A second fabric can be added to make a border. Chintz, a cotton fabric that is frequently glazed, was one of the fashionable materials used in wholecloth quilts. It is the inherent beauty of this printed cloth—featuring large-scale arborescent designs, exotic birds, and fruits—that supplies the decorative elements to these bedcovers. The actual quilting is quite plain. Parallel and crossed lines travel through peonies, peacocks, and pomegranates. Crosshatching, diamonds, basket weaves—all stitched on point—and elongated shells, chevrons, and herringbone patterns appear throughout this period.

It is the inherent beauty of this printed cloth— featuring large-scale arborescent designs, exotic birds, and fruits—that supplies the decorative elements to these bedcovers.

LE PETIT OISEAU ROUGE, A wholecloth quilt created from a decorative French toile tablecloth. Made by the author, 2007.

Wholecloth Quilting Patterns
1810s–1830s

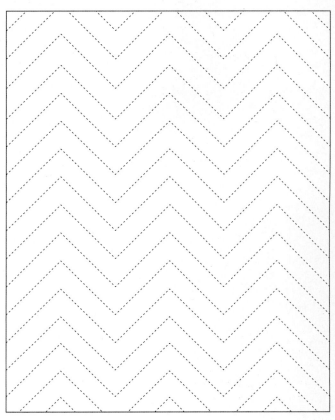

Women were sewing not only plain and simple patterns but fancy quilting designs too. The white-on-white wholecloth style is an example of elaborate design and fine, elegant stitching created by skillful needlewomen. This quilt style can be identified by its white stitching on white fabric. Unlike the beauty of the versions using lovely print fabrics, the beauty of the wholecloth white-on-white style depends on the decorative quality of the quilting motifs. The white-on-white quilts incorporate a wide variety of design elements. Many of the patterns imitate seventeenth- and eighteenth-century British crewel embroidery. These Jacobean designs include naturalistic stems but with unnatural flowers based on exotic and imaginary botany. Feathers abound in every shape, from uncomplicated to complex, multipart arrangements. Although these motifs can be laid out in a variety of ways, typically a medallion set was used. The center area may contain a vessel of fanciful flowers surrounded by borders of geometric shapes and botanical forms. The central design can be a single figure or an arrangement of many motifs framed by feathered swags, wreaths, and undulating vines. Additional stitching techniques often enhance the dimensional quality of these early treasures. Stippling, a background filler of close, tiny stitches, causes the larger stitched motifs to stand out. Stuffed work, a raised design area that includes additional batting, brings designs into even higher relief than that of the background areas.

RENAISSANCE, an example of a white-on-white wholecloth quilt with a characteristic central design of intricate floral forms with meandering branches extending from a vessel. Made by the author, 1998.

White-on-White Wholecloth
Design Elements 1810s–1830s

STRIPPY QUILTS

Another quilt style popular during the early part of the century is the vertical column layout called "strippy quilts." Broad strips of fabric appear as plain rows or alternate with pieced blocks, all with a vertical orientation. Like the magnificently printed wholecloth versions, strippy quilts of this era are generally made from beautifully printed fabrics. Their quilting is plain. It is the beauty of the fabric that gives these bedcovers their decorative style. The same overall geometric patterns found stitched into wholecloth quilts, as well as the less-elaborate border designs of the era, appear on strippy quilts. The entire surface can be covered with just one pattern, or every other strip can be quilted in a different fashion.

Strippy-Style Quilting Patterns 1810s–1830s

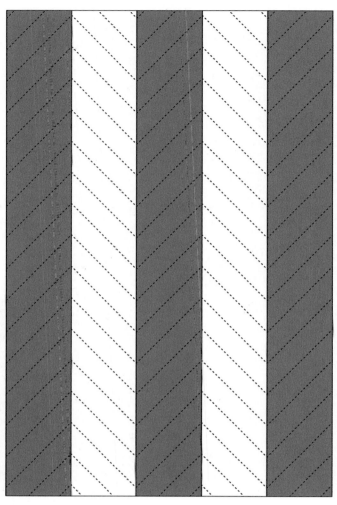

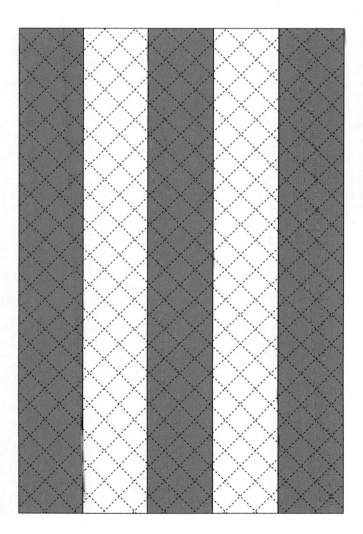

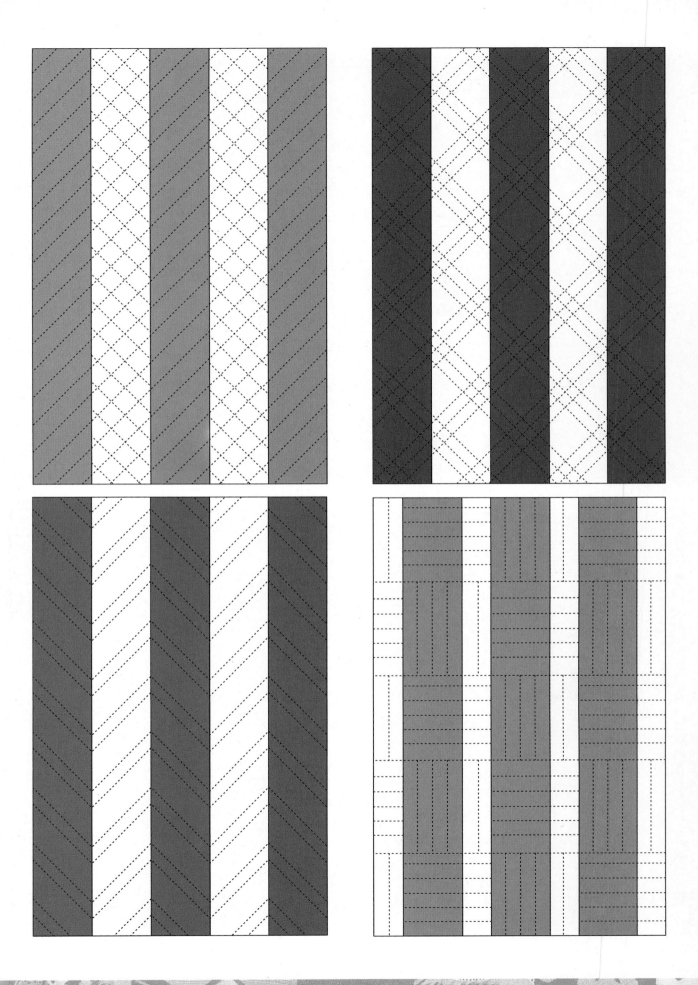

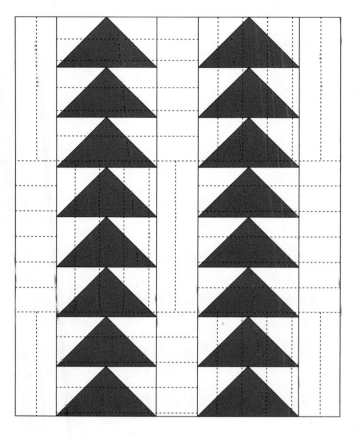

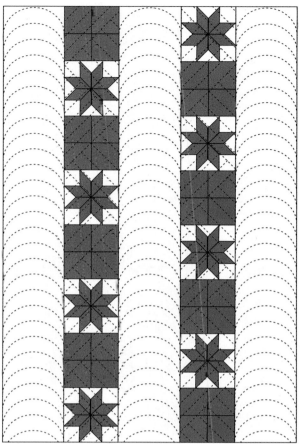

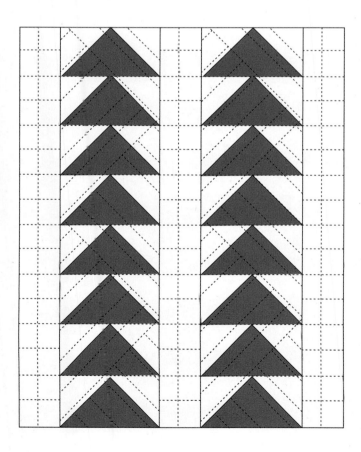

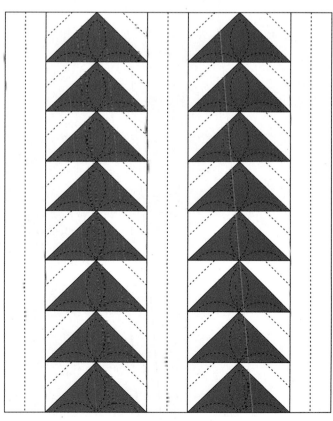

MEDALLION QUILTS

The framed center medallion set was another quilt style seen at this time. It is based on a dominant central design surrounded by significant borders. This style can range from a small center square surrounded by a series of pieced borders of triangles, diamonds, and squares, to a large, botanically inspired design framed by wide floral borders. Small stars and cutout chintz appliqué designs occupy many setting squares and triangles of the Star of Bethlehem (also referred to as Lone Star) quilt pattern. The background of this organized mosaic medallion is stitched with geometric filler patterns or feather and floral design elements.

MADDER ROOT, A classic flowering-tree framed center medallion quilt featuring cutout chintz and machine appliqué techniques. Made by the author, 1997.

A flowering tree that celebrates life and nature, a popular late-eighteenth-century neoclassical design, or a vase or urn of multi-colored flowers frequently appears as the central focus and illustrates the cutout chintz method of appliqué. Today, this technique is called *Broderie Perse*; intriguing birds and intricate flowery designs were cut from beautifully printed and expensive fabrics, including chintz, and artfully arranged and appliquéd, using fine embroidery stitches, onto plain muslin backgrounds. The white background of these detailed center panels is typically closely quilted in geometric patterns of crosshatching, parallel lines, and chevrons.

Examples of Quilting Patterns for the Star of Bethlehem 1810s–1830s

Background and Border Quilting Patterns for Medallion Quilts 1810s–1830s

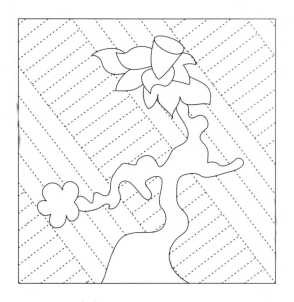

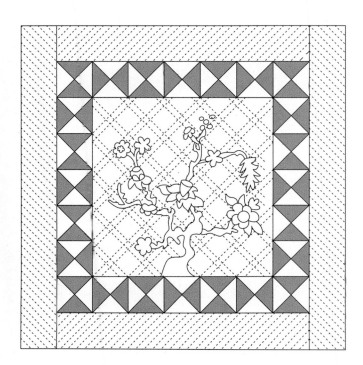

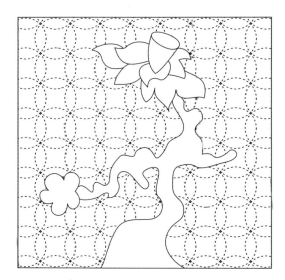

MOSAIC QUILTS

Mosaic piecework (also called one-patch design) is an overall arrangement of a single geometric shape. Fabric design and color placement make the hexagons, shells, diamonds, triangles, and squares appear as a uniform pattern or a haphazard arrangement. Organizing the color scheme and manipulating the print in this repetitive piecing will control the visual outcome. Either way, the overall result is a mosaic of piecework. The patchwork pieces are usually small and plainly quilted. Quilters in the early nineteenth century often sewed through the middle of the patch or stitched concentric shapes.

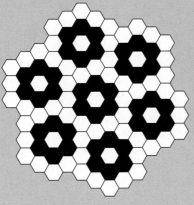

Hexagon Patchwork

The six-sided mosaic pattern known today as Grandmother's Flower Garden was called "hexagons and honey-comb patch-work" when first printed in *The Lady's Book* (later known as *Godey's Lady's Book and Magazine*) in January 1835. This monthly periodical was intended to amuse, enlighten, and educate women. It covered a very wide array of topics, including health, hygiene, fashion, recipes and remedies, literary compositions, and fancy needlework and handicrafts. Early additions even included scientific features on mineralogy and plans for home building.

Mosaic Quilting Patterns
1810s–1830s

STITCHING PATTERNS FOR BLOCKS AND OVERALL DESIGNS

By 1840, the block-style format was emerging as other quilt styles began to fade. This style took on many forms. Quiltmakers of this period combined all the previous quilt styles by alternating pieced blocks with plain blocks, pairing pieced blocks with other pieced blocks, and adding sashing between blocks. The multiple pieced borders of the classic framed center medallion and strippy quilts became separate blocks. Mosaic designs were organized into overall quilt patterns, such as the Irish Chain. The large elaborate central cutout chintz appliqué designs became less-complex individual blocks.

How did needlewomen of this time quilt the block-style quilts? As hand quilters, they knew the difficulty of stitching through multiple seam allowances. Generally they avoided these bulky areas by sewing next to them, not directly through them. In quilts from this era, the quilting lines usually did not follow the overall geometry of the patchwork. Stitched patterns moved across the blocks and paid little attention to the patchwork design. Stitching across a square was more typical than was outlining the area. Following the outline of every patch, either in the seamline or next to it, was rare. Filling a patched surface with stitches parallel to a seamline was much more usual and expected.

Some typical patchwork designs of the day include the hourglass, square-in-a-square, square-on-point, eight-pointed star, nine-patch, flying geese, and half-square triangles. The simplicity of these pieced blocks is echoed in the many unremarkable and utilitarian designs stitched on them: parallel straight lines, crosshatch, diamonds, scallops, shells, and interlocking circles.

Patterns and Overall Designs for Pieced Blocks 1810s–1830s

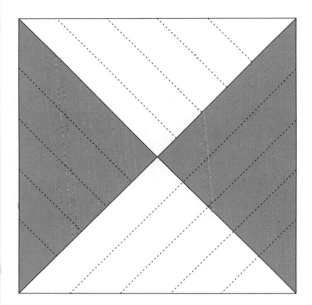

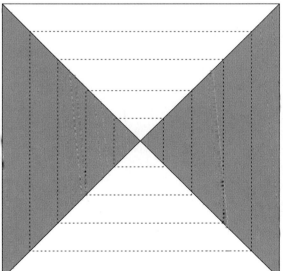

Design Elements 1810s–1830s

Laurel Leaf in Design Elements

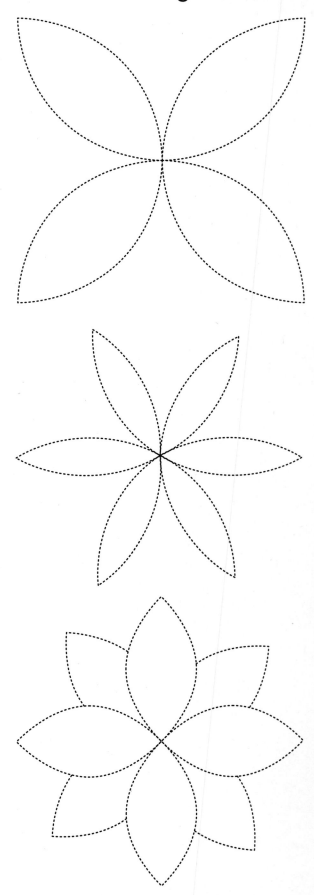

Laurel Leaf Design

One design that was used in a wide variety of places is the laurel leaf. This pointy oval leaf is also referred to as a pumpkin seed. One leaf can stand alone, or if many are strung together they form a chain, and when four are placed on a diagonal axis a quatrefoil is created. This shape can stand alone or be surrounded by a diamond or square. Six leaves form a conventionalized image of a flower. This leaf is a most versatile curved pattern.

Basic Laurel Leaf

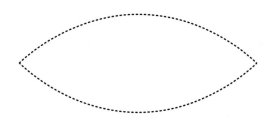

Laurel Leaf in Sashing and Borders

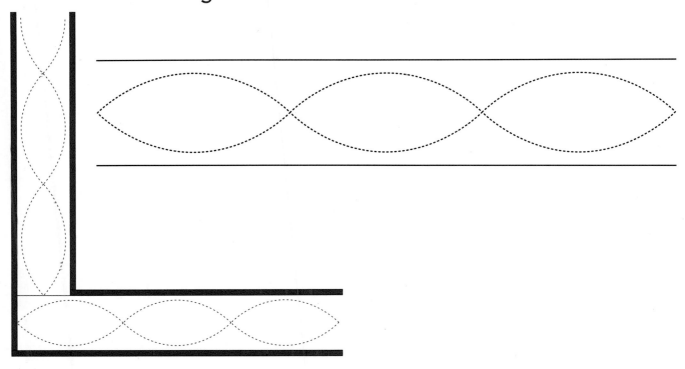

ALTERNATE BLOCKS, SASHINGS, AND BORDERS

Simple geometric patterns were frequently stitched on the beautifully printed textiles used for alternate blocks, sashings, and borders. Elaborate quilting motifs would be obscured by the fanciful fabric print. Although not common, solid (unprinted) fabric does appear in setting blocks, sashings, and borders from this period. Sunflowers, feathered circles, laurels, and vines backed by geometric filler patterns are good design choices for quilting these areas.

Patchwork and Patterns for Alternate Blocks 1810s–1830s

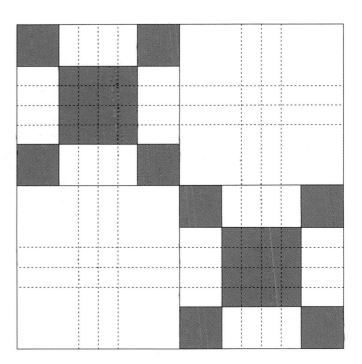

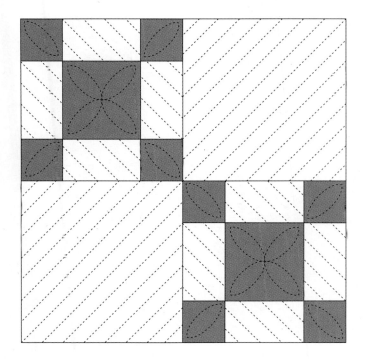

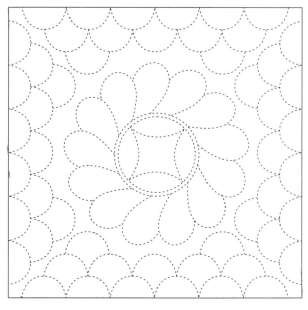

Design Elements for Alternate Blocks 1810s–1830s

Sashing and Border Patterns 1810s–1830s

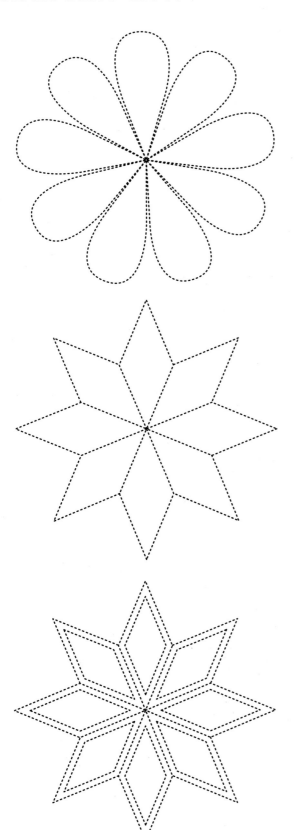

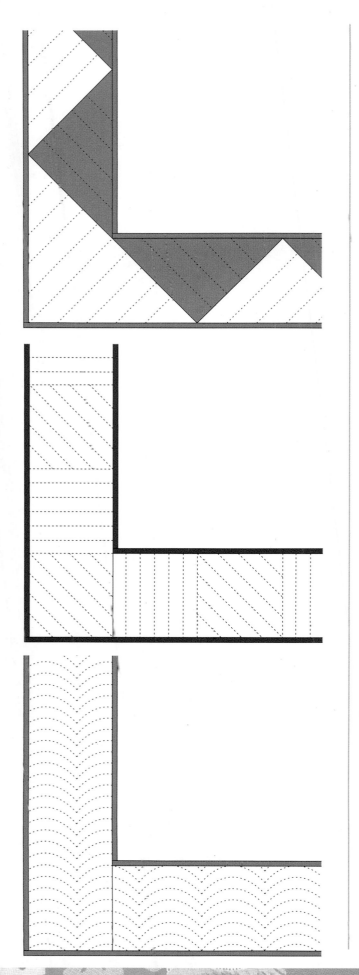

Feathered Border Designs
1810s–1830s

Example of Alternate and Setting Block Design 1810s–1830s

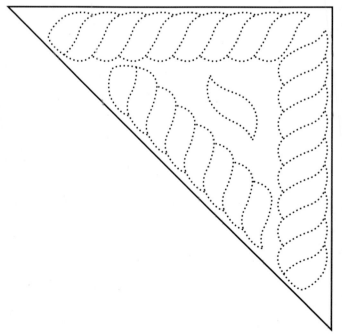

SUMMARY FOR 1810s–1830s QUILTING

The key to creating an early-nineteenth-century feel is stitching a lot of close diagonal lines and filling every space. And remember, lines can change direction at any time.

One household invention that eased the burdens of domestic life was the sewing machine, the first domestic appliance for women.

Sentiments and Signatures. Groups of women made friendship quilts with repeated patchwork blocks as a gesture of friendship, love, and remembrance. The blocks provided a place for each woman to communicate her good wishes to the recipient. These love-filled quilts represented a special bond between the makers and the beneficiary. The expressive cursive writings found on these treasures are full of lovely loops and fluid flourishes. The quilting is plain.

By 1840, the geometric design elements used by quiltmakers had begun to appear as repetitive pieced and appliqué blocks. After 1850, the wholecloth quilt and framed center medallion format fell out of fashion. The overall patterning of straight lines gave way to enhanced artistic expression in quilting motifs. *Godey's Lady's Book and Magazine* offered both old and new "Designs for Quilting" in December 1859 and January 1860.

In the mid-nineteenth century, quilting became an important decorative element. Some of these designs undoubtedly were inspired by nature, as gardening had evolved into almost a domestic cult. Realistic and stylized flowers became very popular design elements for quiltmakers. Roses, carnations, hollyhocks, daisies, bluebells, and forget-me-nots all found their way into appliqué and quilting patterns. One could say quilting was in full bloom.

The Industrial Revolution of the nineteenth century was a time of significant social change, economic growth, and technological progress. The period after the Civil War (1861–1865) brought great new inventions to all aspects of life. One household invention that eased the burdens of domestic life was the sewing machine, the first domestic appliance for women. Elias Howe Jr. was granted a patent for a sewing machine on September 10, 1846, and is generally recognized as the inventor of the machine. However, it was Isaac Singer who really enabled women to own the machines. After enhancing Howe's machine, Singer began to sell his improved version on easy terms. By 1865, Singer's installment-plan marketing scheme had put sewing machines within reach of women throughout America. It has been suggested that as many as 10% of all quilts made between 1865 and 1900 had some machine work in the piecing, appliqué, binding, or quilting. Even if women resisted using this contraption to make quilts, they could use it for other formerly time-consuming household sewing. This timesaving machine freed women to pursue leisurely activities such as quiltmaking.

Geometric Overall Designs from *Godey's Lady's Book and Magazine*, 1859–1860

LEMOYNE STAR, named after brothers Pierre and Jean Baptiste LeMoyne, who directed early French colonization along the Mississippi River near New Orleans. The popular red and green combination of the mid-1800s, often seen in appliqué quilts, is represented here in piecework. Made by the author, 2007.

to making quilts solely from gathered scraps of fabric but were able to buy materials specifically to make them.

The tastes of Britain's Queen Victoria dictated the designs incorporated into the decorative arts during her reign (1837–1901). Everything from bracelets to buildings was decorated with classical designs and interpretations of historical styles. Every space was filled with images that reflected the owner's interests and desires. Feathered designs, stitched throughout the Victorian era, twisted and flowed into every shape to fill every type of space. By 1880, perhaps as a reaction against high Victorian style, the Arts and Crafts and aesthetic movements had their beginnings.

PIECED BLOCKS

The pieced patterns of the early nineteenth century became more complicated. Simple nine-patches became double nine-patches, stars gained sawtooth edges, and single triangles were trimmed with numerous tiny triangles. Multiple blocks of equal size were placed in different settings: side by side for an overall pattern, with sashing, and alternating with plain blocks. Quiltmakers began using the diagonal set by placing blocks on point so the design moved diagonally across the surface of the quilt. Two-color quilts emerged. Indigo-blue-and-white and Turkey-red-and-white were both popular combinations.

The quilting lines in the pieced blocks from this period rarely follow the actual geometric components of each shape. The quilting designs are stitched across seamlines and often in concentric images.

Many factors led to the change in popular quilt styles during this period. A huge quantity and variety of inexpensive fabric was produced and marketed in the United States, while the westward migration of a quarter of a million people across the United States helped spread ideas and quilt patterns. Although many fabrics were available, quilt patterns were not yet being marketed. People were willing to try new things, and individual interpretation and artistic expression made for a wide range of pattern variations. The emerging middle class had more leisure time to experiment and explore new crafts. The transcontinental railway system was completed in 1869, and this meant a tremendous increase in the availability of goods—including machine-made blankets—to everyone. Quiltmakers were not confined

Geometric Quilting Designs for Pieced Blocks 1840s–1870s

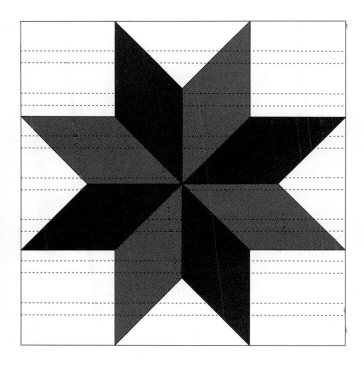

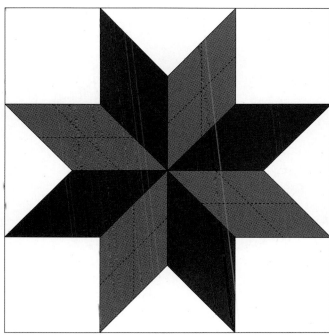

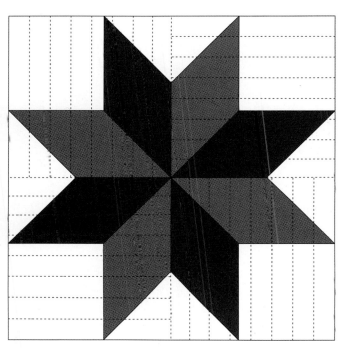

Design Elements for Circular
Patchwork Blocks 1840s–1870s

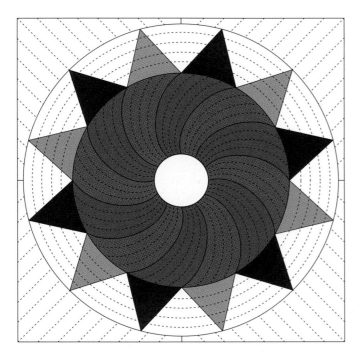

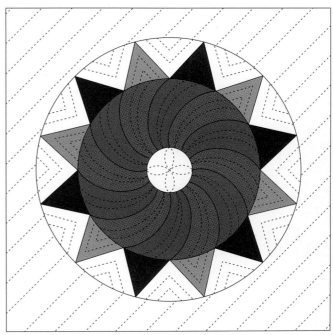

Combinations of Geometric Quilting with Design Elements for Pieced Blocks 1840s–1870s

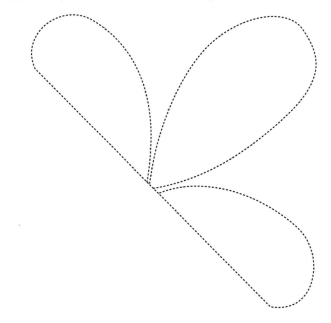

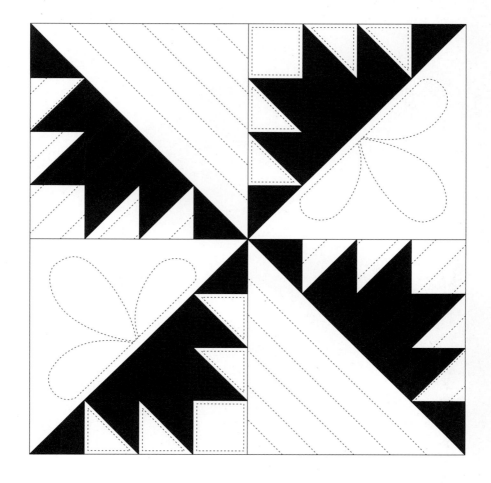

APPLIQUÉ BLOCKS

Appliqué blocks of this period exhibit a great deal of individual creativity. Some quilts feature simple, flat, generic flowers made in a red-and-green combination repeated in all the blocks on a white background. Others, like the superbly executed Baltimore Album quilts, are complex, multihued collages of extreme artistry. The laurel leaf, popular and versatile as a quilting design, developed into an appliqué pattern, and baskets were now pieced rather than cut from one fabric and appliquéd onto a background.

The prints on the numerous available fabrics were generally smaller in scale and lent themselves to small geometric patchwork patterns and the individual elements of a floral appliqué. Rather than cutting out the entire flower from expensive chintz, the quiltmaker cut individual parts of the bloom from separate fabrics.

Since early in the nineteenth century, women had collected favorite poetry, illustrations, and autographs and placed them in scrapbooks. Album quilts could be an offspring of this activity. These sentimental treasures were usually made of appliqué blocks contributed by many women or were the result of one individual celebrating or memorializing a special event.

Appliqué quilts were quilted using "echo quilting," following the outline of the shape and filling large shapes with concentric lines. Elements of the actual appliqué can be repeated in the composition, and images of flowers (stylized or real) are interspaced among the blocks. Circles, laurel leaves, and shells can also fill odd spaces between appliqués. Just as parallel lines were used at the beginning of the century, they continued to appear on appliqué quilts from this period. The lines are close together and travel across the entire quilt. Sometimes the grids avoid the appliqués, while other times lines travel across the entire appliqué, having no regard to the actual fabric design. Lines change direction, sometimes in planned areas such as corners and sometimes seemingly at will.

Since early in the nineteenth century, women had collected favorite poetry, illustrations, and autographs and placed them in scrapbooks. Album quilts could be an offspring of this activity.

Not like the rose
Shall our friendship whither
But like the evergreen
Live forever

Examples of Appliqué Block
Quilting 1840s–1870s

Design Elements for Appliqué Blocks 1840s–1870s

APPLIQUÉ BLOCK QUILTING

In quilts from this period, the backgrounds of simple appliqué motifs can be quilted with filler patterns of closely stitched diagonal parallel lines, crosshatch, or double- and triple-line quilting. Alternate blocks can contain simple or ornate patterns. Elaborate appliqué versions can include hearts, flowers, and the princess (or prince's) feather with its many variations. A conscious effort to design something highly sophisticated is evident in many of the appliqué quilts of this era, and their corresponding quilting designs contain the same amount of artistry. Tucking in a floral motif here or a heart there played to the Victorian desire to fill every space and to add symbolism, superstition, and sentimentality.

Inspiration for quilting designs came from a variety of sources, but probably none as exciting as nature. The fanatical interest in gardening had women stitching flowers onto countless quilts. New varieties of flowers were discovered, developed, imported, and widely planted throughout the United States. The first fragrant moss roses were imported from France in 1854. The peak of cultivation of old English tulips by Victorian gardeners was about 1850. It is not surprising that botanical forms frequently fill the alternate blocks between pieced and appliqué designs. All the space is filled. Classical arrangements of multiple blooms, leafy sprays of flowers, and feathered wreaths with grid- and floral-filled centers all materialize on the quilts of this period. The flexible feather form is worked into almost any shape and takes on many, many variations. A background grid pattern completes the Victorian ideal of filling every space and adds emphasis to the botanical shapes.

Patterns for Alternate Blocks
1840s–1870s

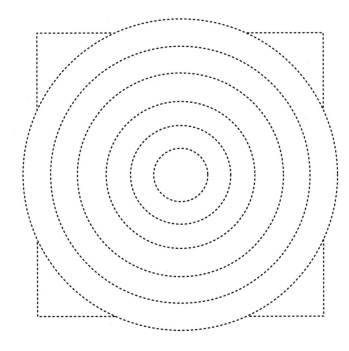

More Design Elements for Alternate and Appliqué Blocks 1840s–1870s

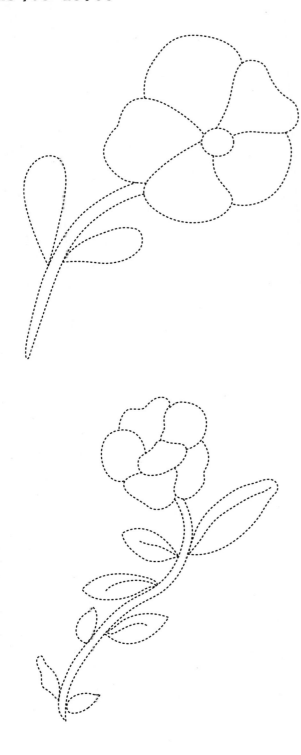

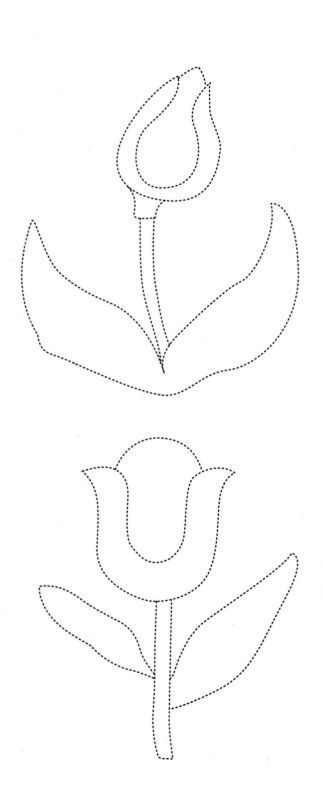

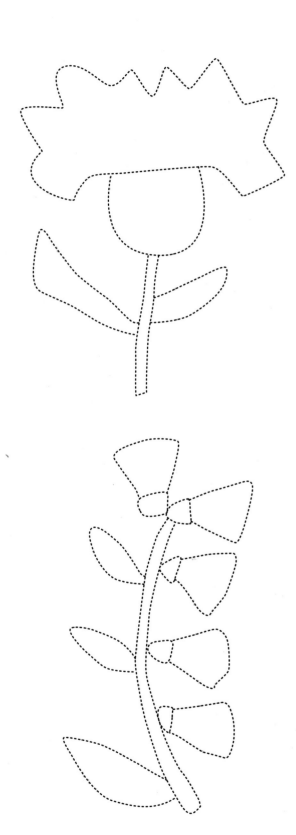

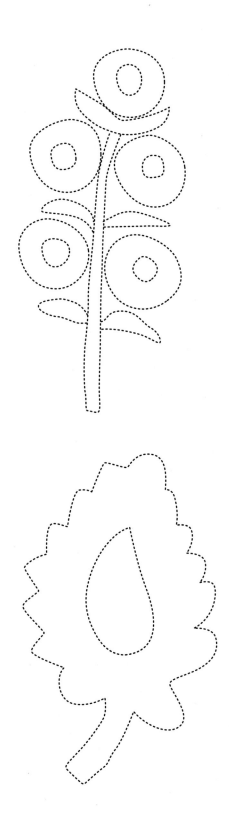

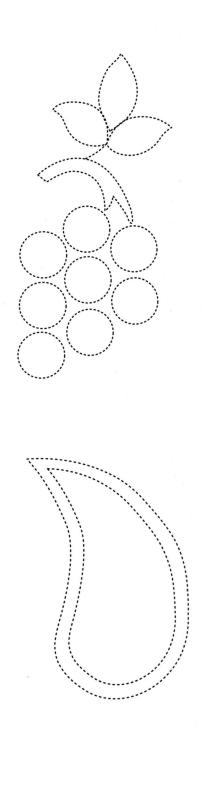

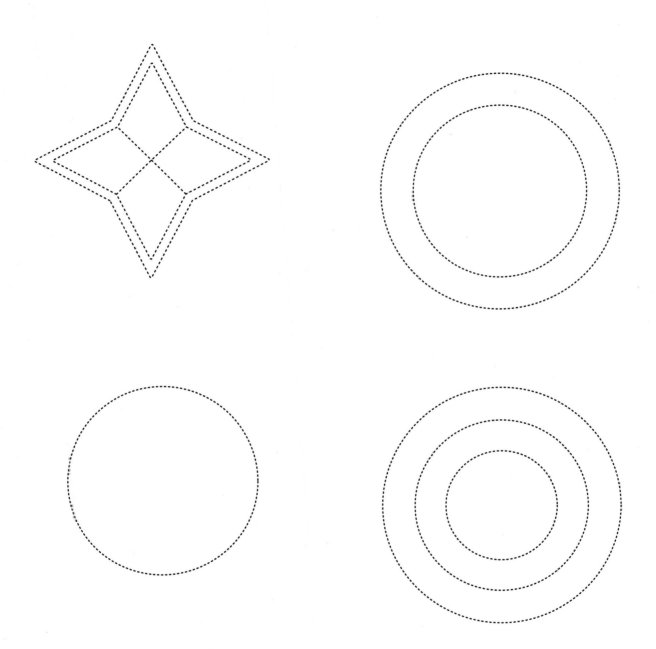

Feathered Designs for Alternate
Blocks 1840s–1870s

Combinations of Feathered
and Design Elements
1840s–1870s

SASHINGS AND BORDERS

Quilters added sashings of many widths between blocks. Many pieced quilts had sashings and no borders. Sashings were simply quilted with parallel lines and cross-hatch or with a narrow row of feathers and simple cable.

Bold swags and floral vines were appliquéd onto many borders during this era. They were often surrounded by closely stitched quilted chevrons and diagonal parallel lines that changed direction at each corner or in the middle of each side. Outlining each shape by stitching in-the-ditch was rarely seen at this time.

The feathered vines and cables used as quilting designs were seldom designed or drawn out in advance. As with appliqué borders, there was little attempt to continue the design around the corner or even to turn each corner the same way. The result was a different design treatment in each corner, or the design ran off the edge at each corner. To avoid this visual outcome, a feathered wreath could be placed in each corner to terminate the feathered vine.

Sashing and Border Elements and Patterns 1840s–1870s

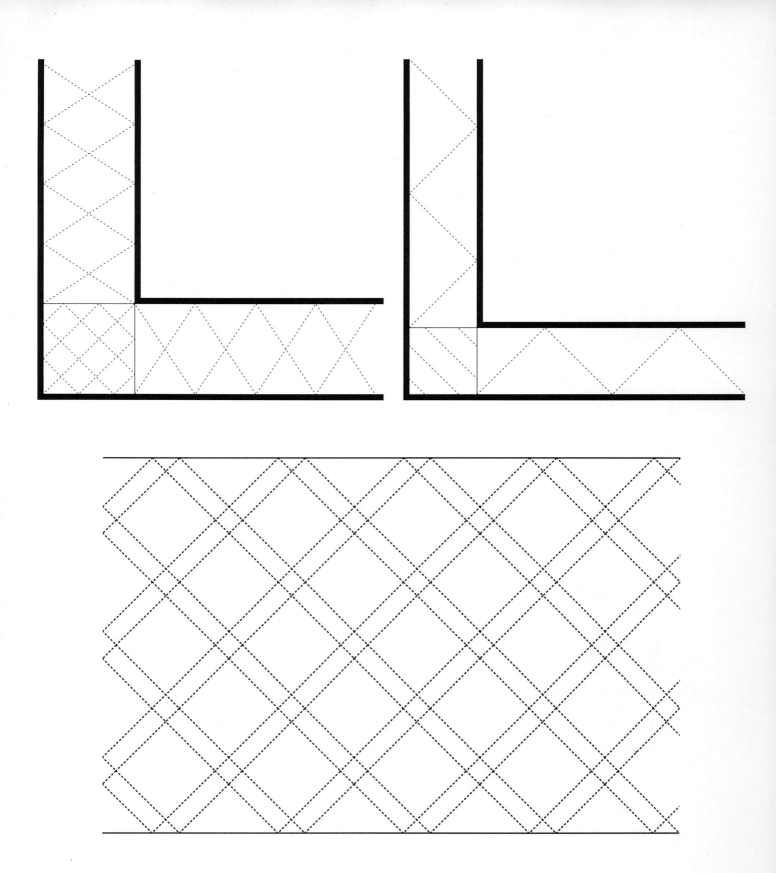

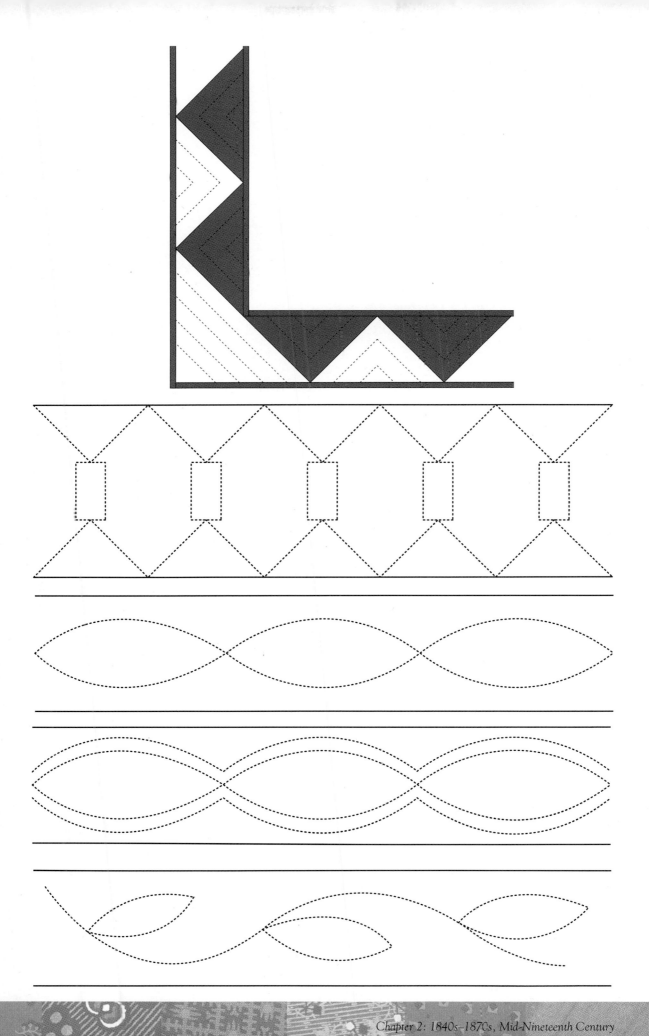

Swag Border Elements and Patterns
1840s–1870s

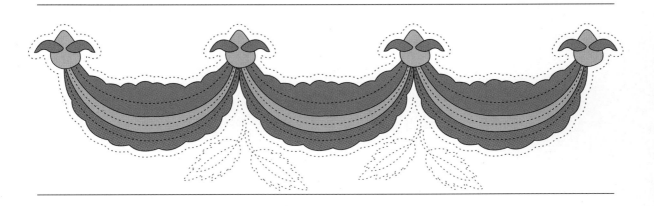

SUMMARY FOR 1840s–1870s QUILTING

For a mid-century look, remember that any line or shape can become showy when enhanced by feathers. Also remember the popularity of botanical forms and of filling every space with straight grids and curved images.

KANSAS TROUBLES, Made by the author, 1998.

The modern woman had many new developments and distractions to fill her time. These new developments affected every aspect of life, from entertainment to medicine to fastenings.

Mass production during the second phase of the Industrial Revolution (1865–1900) led to a huge array of available consumer goods. By the end of the nineteenth century, factory-made blankets and bedspreads had become very popular. This resulted in a sharp decline in quiltmaking. It was no longer necessary to spend numerous hours cutting, piecing, and quilting blankets for the family. Local stores in towns and cities offered affordable manufactured goods, and free rural delivery made them available in farming and ranching communities. Mass-produced bedcovers were inexpensive and readily available.

Previously, in the early Victorian Age, women strove to be admired as genteel, delicate females. She pinched her waist and shielded her complexion from the sun and was ashamed of showing any appetite for food. She made herself interesting by having fainting-fits and hysterics whenever anything went wrong. Now that sort of young woman is extinct and in her place is the cycling girl, the golfing girl, the yachting girl, the girl who drives a motor-boat, drinks highballs and carries a cigarette case. What is in vogue now is an active woman of strong character.

The Cosmopolitan Magazine, November 1904

The modern woman had many new developments and distractions to fill her time. These new developments affected every aspect of life, from entertainment to medicine to fastenings. The first movie theater opened in Los Angeles, Crayola crayons were marketed, and aspirin was developed. The first zipper, safety pin, and paper clip were patented. Endless household chores became easier. The feather duster, electric flatiron, and canned fruits and meats made their debut. Edison developed the practical light bulb, W.H. Carrier developed air conditioning, and the Wright brothers flew at Kitty Hawk. Ford Motor Company was established, and although it produced only 1,708 automobiles in 1903, the mass-production, mass-marketing phenomenon would soon increase individual mobility throughout the land. Increasing numbers of women were entering colleges and professional fields and taking jobs outside the home. The idea of the weekend was becoming a popular notion. Leisure time was filled with activities other than creating beautiful bedcovers.

FRIENDSHIP STAR, The block, first published as "Braced Star" in *Ladies Art Circle* in 1889, later appeared in *Hearth and Home Magazine* in 1907. Made by author, 2002.

Women wanted new and modern furnishings for their homes. The authorities on fashion and home decorating were the periodicals of the day, and editorials and articles covered every phase of women's lives.

Women wanted new and modern furnishings for their homes. The authorities on fashion and home decorating were the periodicals of the day, and editorials and articles covered every phase of women's lives. In *The Cosmopolitan Magazine*, November 1904, a subscription advertisement for *The Delineator* claimed that valuable information was provided in the monthly magazine, which covered a woman's "home; household duties; the care, amusement and education of her children; the science of her kitchen; as well as her own hours of rest and recreation." These magazines suggested that they belonged in every cultured home and offered appropriate advice and activities for the modern woman.

There is no mention of patchwork or quilting in the May 1907 issue of *The Modern Priscilla* magazine, an illustrated monthly journal devoted to art needlework, home decoration, furnishing, and other household matters. In the late nineteenth and early twentieth centuries, using quilts to decorate the home would have been considered quaint and old-fashioned.

Crazy patch and redwork embroidery became popular novelty needlework techniques and made their way into quilts. A crazy patch quilt consists of blocks assembled by sewing pieces onto a base of muslin or other fabric. Very little, if any, quilting is required. The construction technique adds strength and stability to the work. Many crazy patch quilts have no batting. In the 1880s, at the height of the craze, showy crazy patch parlor throws were created with lush velvets, taffetas, satins, brocades, fancy cottons, and woolens. Many contain commemorative ribbons. Women decorated the surfaces abundantly with numerous and intricate silk embroidery stitches and skillfully painted images. By 1900, the fabrics being used to create them were simple wools and cottons, but they still were decorated with embroidery, although the stitches were now sewn with cotton floss and were much simpler and less varied.

FLYING GEESE, This popular patchwork, with its characteristic 1880's color scheme, suggests a bygone era. Made by the author, 2007.

DRUNKARD'S PATCHWORK, The Ladies Art Company published this layout for Drunkard's Path at the turn of the twentieth century. This quilt is a copy of one owned by the author. Made by the author, 2007.

ZIGZAG, An example of a strippy quilt,
the four-patch blocks are placed in a zigzag setting.
Made by the author, 2001.

Redwork Embroidery Quilting Designs 1880s–1910s

Redwork embroidery, named after the colorfast Turkey red cotton floss used to stitch the majority of them, was popular from 1885 to 1925. Design themes were varied. Some embroidered blocks contain simple floral, bird, and animal designs stitched onto muslin squares. Others are elaborate depictions of buildings and famous people. Nursery rhymes were also a popular subject. The intended focus was on the stitched image, and even though these blocks contain open spaces of plain cloth, the quilting is very plain. Basic grids of crosshatch, diamonds, and simple diagonal lines go through the blocks. Sometimes the quilting is stitched through the embroidered image, and sometimes it stops at the embroidery's edge. Many redwork bedcovers are finished as coverlets and not quilted at all.

Generally, quilts at the turn of the twentieth century were made from simple forms, for utilitarian purposes. Tied quilts appeared at this time. Quilters had long abandoned the fine finishing details of cording, stippling, and stuffed work. The elegant and refined double- and triple-line stitching on mid-century quilts was replaced with single-line grids similar to the overall designs sewn onto early wholecloth quilts.

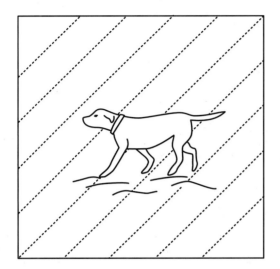

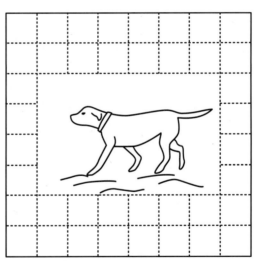

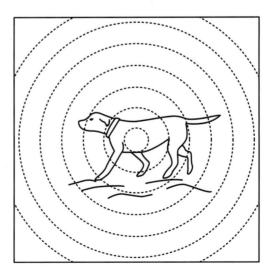

Fan Quilting Designs 1880s–1910s

Functional, not ornamental, quilting was the usual and expected stitching. Generally, there were fewer stitching lines per square foot. Elaborate quilting was seen at this time, but it is perhaps most attributed to older women who had been making quilts during the middle of the century, when they used their hand-sewing skills to create quilted masterpieces.

Individual craftsmanship suffered when the sewing machine and ready-to-wear clothes freed women to take up other endeavors. By 1900, the sewing machine had ceased to be a status symbol, as most families now had one. It was handwork that was now seen as the status symbol. Women who had the luxury of leisure time stitched embroidered details on clothing and household accessories. Waists (blouses), aprons, corset covers, yokes, collars, cuffs, table centerpieces, doilies, belts, and even hats were embellished with handwork. Quilting was too old fashioned for the *The Cosmopolitan Magazine*'s modern "cycling girl."

Two patterns emerged as common overall quilting designs in the late nineteenth century. Fan quilting and hanging diamonds appear on all quilt styles of this period. Fan quilting, also called elbow quilting, is a pattern of concentric arcs. It is comfortable to sew and can be rapidly stitched. The arc is established by pivoting the arm at the elbow. When the pattern is marked on the fabric, the arcs are generally rounded, smooth, and uniform. Arcs resembling the angle of an actual elbow, unevenly spaced and irregular, are more likely to have been stitched freely without the benefit of marking.

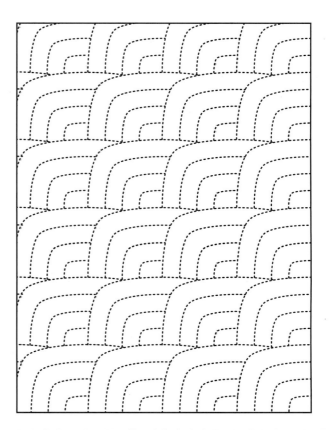

Hanging Diamond Design 1880s–1910s

Hanging diamonds are created when straight parallel lines are stitched from opposite edges in one direction only, from top to bottom or from side to side. A second set of straight parallel lines is added at an angle, in one direction only. The space between the lines can be an equal distance or vary in width.

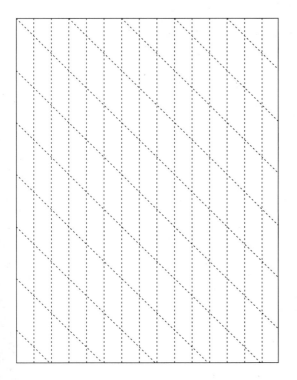 

Overall Pattern 1880s–1910s

Overall designs are a good representative pattern of this era and can be as simple as parallel lines going in one direction and then changing direction across the surface of the quilt.

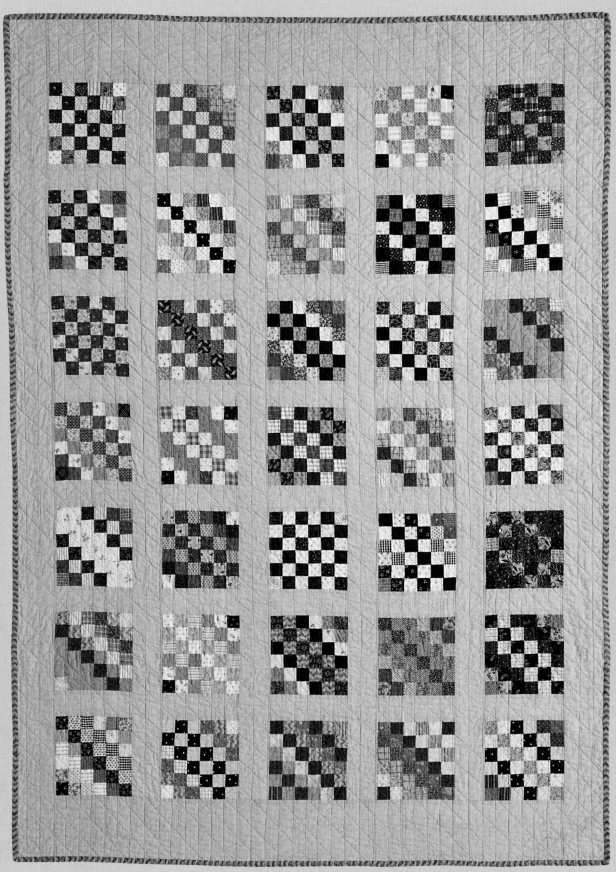

36-PATCH, Inspired by an antique quilt owned by Pamela Roberts Lindsay, the blocks are the result of a friendship group exchange. Assembled and quilted by the author, 2003.

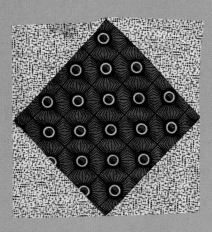

REPEATING PATCHWORK, BLOCK-TO-BLOCK SETS

The variety of pieced patterns increased. The signature quilt style was revived for a time. The sampler quilt, made with separate predominately pieced pattern designs arranged in block format, appeared, while the fancy and elaborate album style disappeared. The complexity of new block designs is evident in patterns such as Drunkards Path, Schoolhouse, and Ocean Wave. Appliqué patterns became simpler. Designs were outlined in quilting stitches, that is, following the individual pieces of the piecing. Some interior parallel lines were added to larger pieces because batting would migrate to the stitching lines, creating flat areas, if sufficient quilting wasn't applied. A quilt made of a patchwork block repeated many times could have different grid patterns stitched on different blocks.

A company in St. Louis offered patterns for patchwork during the late nineteenth century. The Ladies Art Company, which was owned by H.M. Brockstedt and published its first patterns in 1889, published *Diagrams of Quilt, Sofa* and *Pincushion Patterns*. New patterns continued to be added, and by 1922 the catalog contained 458 pieced blocks, 42 appliqué blocks, 37 quilting motifs, 42 embroidery designs, and a variety of crazy patch embroidery stitches. The Ladies Art Company catalog is recognized as being the earliest catalog devoted to quilt patterns and is the first significant collection of patchwork block style designs to appear in print.

Examples of Grid Quilting on Beauregard's Surrounded Quilt 1880s–1910s

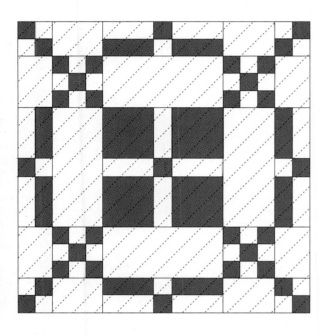

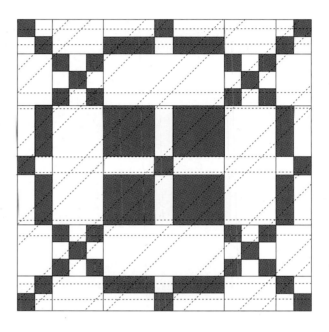

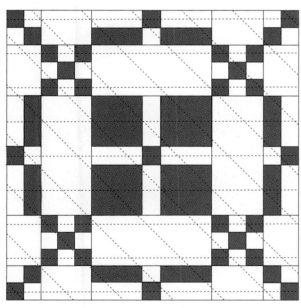

Drunkard's Path Quilting 1880s–1910s

Examples of Designs on Charm Quilts 1880s–1910s

Foundation-pieced blocks such as the Log Cabin and all its variations were assembled on a stabilizing base cloth and required little quilting, if any.

One-patch designs emerged again, as evident in fundraising and charm quilts. The social and economic movements of the period gave women greater freedom and more leisure time than they had ever had before. Women were turning their attention to many causes. The Christian Temperance Union, the American Red Cross, and church needs were favorite causes. Quilts were used as a means to raise funds. Ladies in churches across America created formal organizations to raise money to repair roofs, install carpeting, provide hymnbooks, and build new sanctuaries. Some expanded to include missionary work. Women gathered signatures throughout the community, and the names were embroidered or inked onto quilt tops. People paid for their space on the quilt.

The intent of these quilts was to raise money. Simple one-patch designs were regularly used, as were large pieces of solid muslin on which the embroidered signatures became the motif. Little time was spent on the actual quilting.

One-patch designs also reappeared as charm quilts. This popular style of patchwork used a single geometric shape, such as a square, hexagon, or triangle, and was composed of hundreds of different cotton fabrics. Ideally, no two pieces would be the same. This made for a grand statement at the time and is helpful now in identifying the colors and prints the era's quiltmakers had access to, either through an inherited scrap bag or as new, inexpensive American-made calico fabrics. Charm quilts are essentially albums of fabrics. Simple quilting was used to hold these charm quilts together.

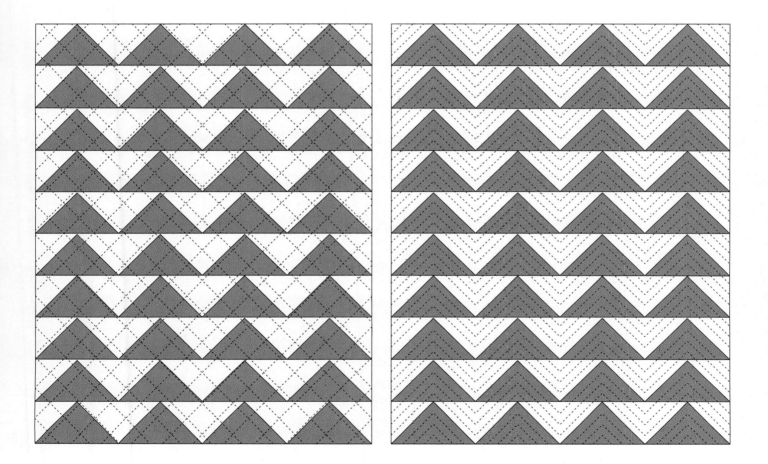

ALTERNATE PLAIN BLOCKS

Alternate blocks could be of printed or unprinted fabric. Even when abundant plain space was present, many quilts from this time period were simply quilted. Alternate blocks contained grids and vague sprawling forms. A fancy motif that enjoyed long-standing popularity, feather designs, remained and occupied a place on quilted treasures.

Basic Quilt Grids for Strippy Quilts 1880s–1910s

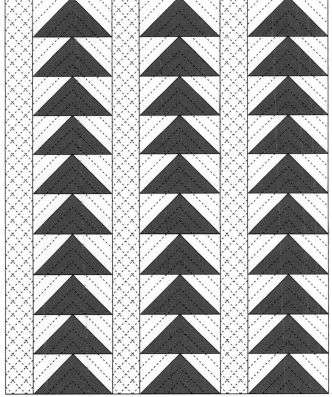

STRIPPY QUILTS

The strippy quilt regained popularity and appeared as strips of fabric between rows of patchwork and as zigzags. The zigzag set develops when every other row of patchwork is sewn starting with a half block. This drops the design down by half. Basic quilt grids and simple shapes are found stitched onto the strippy sets.

SASHINGS AND BORDERS

The decline in the skill of quiltmakers at the turn of the century was nowhere more evident than in the border designs. Corner treatments could be quite rough. Corner designs changed from one to the next on the same quilt. The design was not worked out in advance, and many times all four corners would be different. Cables would run off the edge and start up again on the next side. Generally, the individual elements of the border were not measured first and were not fitted mathematically to the size of the quilt. This hit-or-miss treatment was representative of the times.

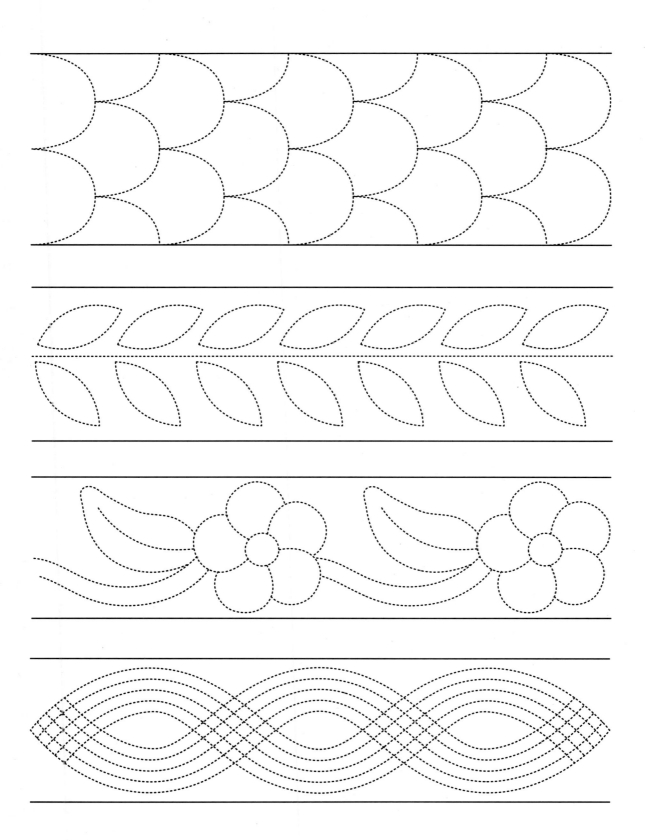

Summary for 1880s–1910s Quilting

The most prevalent quilting designs at the turn of the twentieth century were modest, non-ornamental patterns of functional stitching used to structurally hold fabric layers together. The hanging diamond grid and fan quilting are appropriate quilting patterns for patchwork or appliqué blocks made at this time.

4 *Early Twentieth Century*

A widespread interest in remembering and preserving America's past generations appeared during a time we now call the Colonial Revival.

HOME ARTS

EYES ON STYLE .·. QUILTED PATCHWORK GOES MODERN

The 1920s were a time when farm productivity was up and farm prices were down. For the first time, more Americans were living in cities than in rural areas. There was more social freedom as the middle class grew and prospered. Two developments were essential to this rapid rise of a consumer culture—the automobile and the radio. The radio increased communication and provided entertainment at home. The automobile put a generation on wheels. Henry Ford improved mass-production methods and introduced the assembly line. The demand for efficiency and elimination of waste was the cry of the Efficiency Movement (1890–1932). An ingrained respect for the usefulness of things prevented many from throwing very much away.

A widespread interest in remembering and preserving America's past generations appeared during a time we now call the Colonial Revival. This was when the restoration of Colonial Williamsburg, Virginia, began. Colonial furniture was a popular style in home interiors. Naturally, quilts and coverlets reminded women of bygone eras.

Our interest in replicating the past was not limited to the actual period before the American Revolution. In 1915, Marie Webster wrote a book on the history of quilts. *Quilts: Their Story and How to Make Them* provided a wealth of information about many nineteenth-century quilts and patterns. Even the modern woman was interested in making something her grandmother would have made. In *The Modern Priscilla*, a magazine article (March 1926) declares, "Patchwork's the Thing for Coverlets. Who would have expected the renaissance of the calico quilt to arrive in the midst of the age of jazz!"

The 1920s and 1930s saw the launch of many mail-order quilt pattern businesses. Customers bought patterns directly from a catalog or ordered them through periodicals. Many local newspapers and magazines contained syndicated quilt columns and offered syndicated mail-order patterns. Individual quilting patterns were priced according to size and design. Some designs were offered for sale at 10¢ each, or three for 25¢. Ruby McKim and Anne Orr signed their patterns, but most designers were either anonymous or not real people at all. Imaginary people had names reflecting the nation's interest in the olden days, ancestors, and prosperity—names such as Aunt Martha (a reminder of Martha Washington), Grandma Dexter, Grandmother Clark, and Hope Winslow.

DUDLEY'S AIRPLANE QUILT, Soon after Charles Lindbergh's flight from New York to Paris in 1927, Emma Shackelford Tyrrell of Iowa created a realistic airplane pattern inspired by his plane, *The Spirit of St. Louis*. *The Kansas City Star* newspaper also printed an aircraft pattern sent in by reader Mrs. Otto Prell from Oklahoma. The quilt shown is on display in the historic Dudley House, built in 1892, in Ventura, California. Young Leavitt Dudley was fascinated by flight and created model airplanes to hang in his room. Surely, Leavitt would have loved to have this quilt on his bed. Made by Joan Wilcox Garner and friends as a remembrance of Joan's daughter, Judith Dawn Garner; pattern and design advice by the author, 2003.

SWEET BUTTERFLIES, This cheery appliqué quilt is more elaborately quilted than the grid-covered antique quilt that inspired its construction. Made by the author, 2007.

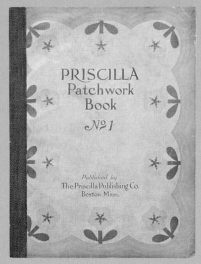

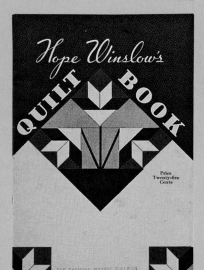

In 1925, *Priscilla Patchwork Book No. 1*, published by The Priscilla Publishing Company of Boston, offered appliqué and pieced designs. The writers acknowledged the beauty of handmade needlework but also suggested a modern approach to creating quilts popular during this Colonial Revival period. This booklet contains an article ("The Making of a Quilt") reminding women that although the previous generation had done the quilting by hand and that the quilting bee had been a popular form of social entertainment, times had changed:

> Nowadays, the work is frequently done on the sewing-machine… When quilting is done on the machine (a necessity in these busy times), a paper bearing the quilting design may be tacked over the quilt, and the stitching done right through paper and quilt. The paper is easily torn away later. Straight-line quilting, in rows crossing each other at right angles or diagonally, is very easily managed on the machine if the quilting attachment is used, for it has an adjustable guiding bar for this purpose.

The United States experienced a nationwide economic depression during the 1930s. But with low-cost fabrics and cheap pattern sources, quilts were being made in even greater numbers. Perhaps for some, the hard times were relieved by making quaint reminders of days gone by. The sewing machine was even more accepted now. Yes, quilts of the 1930s were both hand and machine quilted!

POPULAR DESIGNS

Quiltmakers throughout the 1920s and 1930s made countless quilts, both pieced and appliquéd, and both in modern styles and using patterns with an old-time flavor. Different patterns pleased different tastes and accommodated varying degrees of skill. Three patterns that had widespread appeal and appear in great numbers in quilts from this time period are **Grandmother's Flower Garden, Double Wedding Ring,** and **Dresden Plate.** These patterns can be made from fragments of cloth that include everything from modest recycled feed and flour sacks to lustrous smooth sateen.

Grandmother's Flower Garden
Designs 1920s–1940

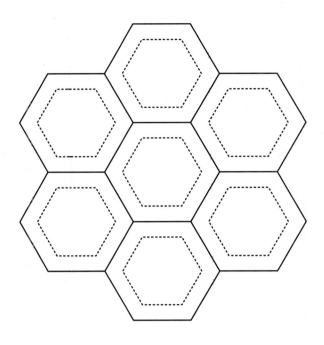

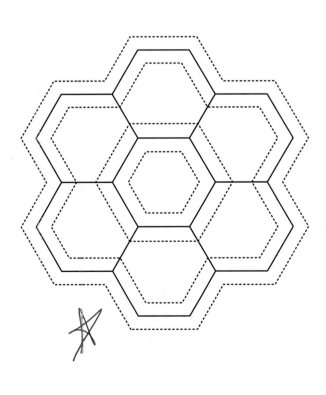

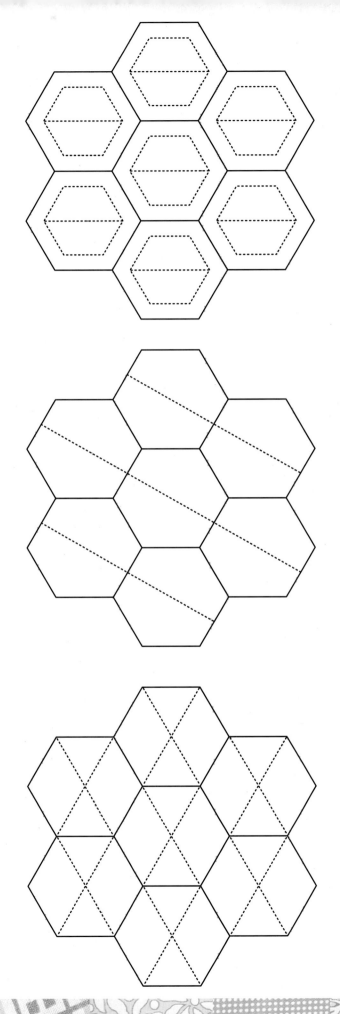

Double Wedding Ring Designs
1920s–1940

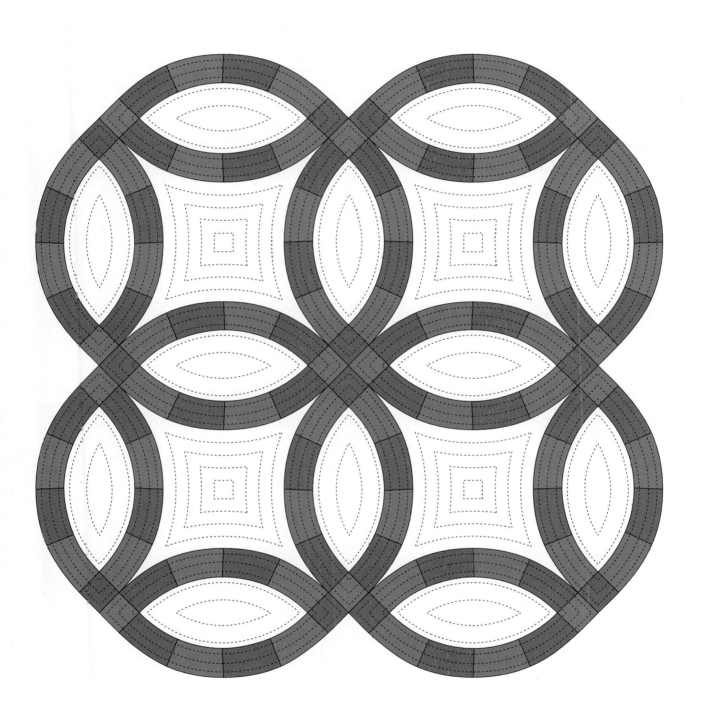

Quilting Designs from the Past

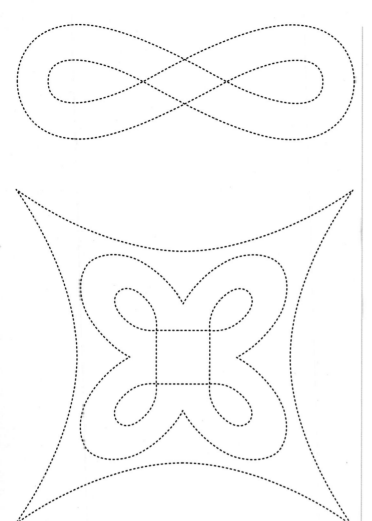

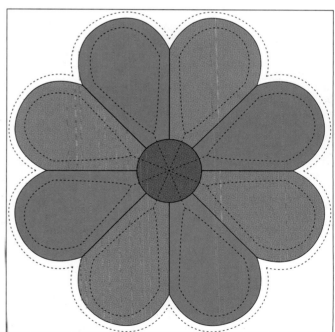

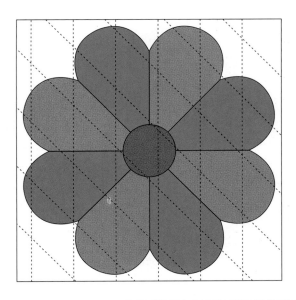

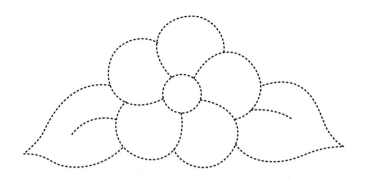

REPEATING BLOCKS

The characteristic style of quilting patchwork by the mid-1920s was "by the piece." In this style, the geometric shapes of the patchwork are recreated by stitching ¼″ away from each seamline that creates the block.

The overall fan design from the turn of the twentieth century continued to be stitched onto bedcovers as well, while the shell pattern became rounder than the elongated version favored at the beginning of the previous century.

Quilting "By the Piece" 1920s–1940

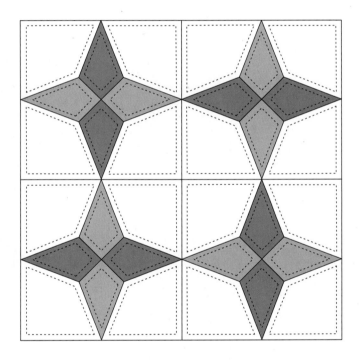

Fan Pattern 1920s–1940

Shell Pattern 1920s–1940

Grid Backgrounds for Appliqué Blocks 1920s–1940

In quilts from this period, open spaces around appliqué and embroidered shapes are filled with a variety of straight lines forming square and diamond grids. The most usual and expected stitching patterns are parallel lines set 1″ apart and crosshatching from ½″ to 1″ apart. Simple to more complex ellipse, square, circle, and half-circle forms can appear between appliqué blocks. Single flowers or groupings of blooms and leaves can surround appliqué and embroidered designs.

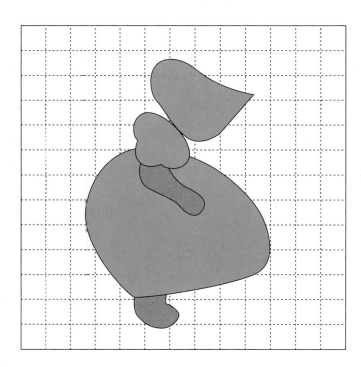

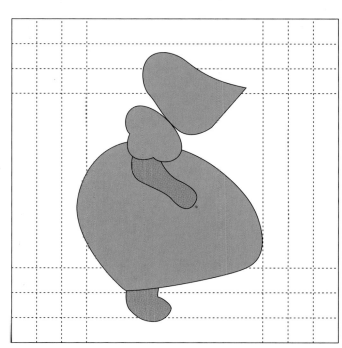

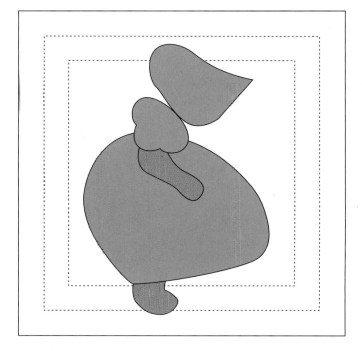

Corner Block Designs for Sashings and Borders 1920s–1940

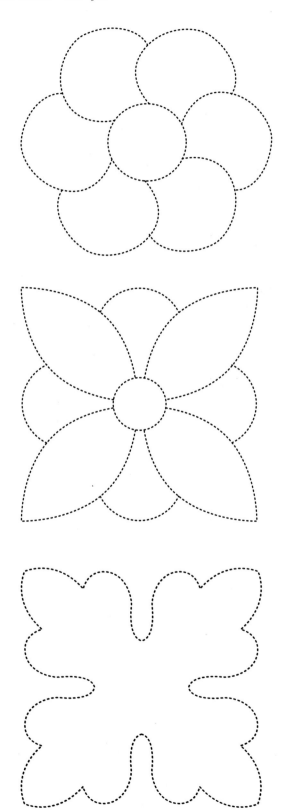

SASHINGS AND BORDERS

Overall designs (those that cover the entire surface of the top) are also found as border designs on quilts from this period. Basic grids, shells, and fans were popular border motifs. Multi-line cable and connecting flora speak to Colonial Revival sensibilities. Small motifs and simplified versions of elaborate ones can be found in the corner blocks of sashings and borders. Border designs include straight and waved feathered plumes, and twisted ropes.

Sashing and Border Designs 1920s–1940

Quilting Designs from the Past

Complementary Block and Border Designs from H. Ver Mehren, 1933

Intricate designs for alternate blocks and setting triangles were skillfully combined with complementary border patterns during this time. A scalloped finished edge adds to the delicacy of the quilting.

MEDALLION QUILTS

The traditional central medallion format of the early nineteenth century returned in the medallion quilts of the twentieth century. Interest in the Colonial Revival movement brought on a resurgence of this once-popular style. The central focus of medallion quilts can range from elaborate compositions of flowers to multiple blocks of butterflies. The medallion-set quilt, stitched in light, bright, cheery fabrics, was simply quilted with grid and cable patterns. More involved quilting designs appear as feathered and floral motifs. Any of the stitching patterns presented in this chapter could be stitched onto medallion quilts of this period.

SUMMARY FOR 1920s–1940 QUILTING

The usual and expected quilting style for patchwork from this period is by the piece, which follows each geometric shape ¼″ on both sides of the seamline. Appliqué motifs are surrounded by crosshatching—crossed straight lines ½″ to 1″ apart.

RESIZING THE DESIGN

Your quilt top is complete, and you have selected appropriate quilting patterns. Before you transfer the designs from the page to the cloth, check their size against the space they will fill. You will probably need to reduce or enlarge the images to fill the space on your quilt. Generally, alternate block, sashing, and border designs float ¼″ to ½″ inside the seamlines surrounding them. Remember to add this amount to the design area measurements. Divide the size you need by the motif's current size. Use a proportional scale or follow these simple steps to resize the image on a copy machine.

To resize a design, you need to have 2 numbers:

1. Measure the printed design on the page and consider the space beyond if the motif is to float. This is the area of printed design.

2. Measure the quilting area that you want the design to fill on your quilt. This is the quilt area to be filled.

ENLARGING THE DESIGN
1. Design needs to fill an 8″ quilt area.
2. Printed design comfortably fills a 3″ printed area.
3. 8 (quilt area to be filled) ÷ 3 (area of printed design) = 2.666.
4. Round this number to 2.67.
5. Move the decimal point 2 places to the right = 267.
6. Enlarge the design 267%.

REDUCING THE DESIGN
1. Design needs to fill a 2″ quilt area.
2. Printed design comfortably fills a 3″ printed area.
3. 2 (quilt area to be filled) ÷ 3 (area of printed design) = 0.666.
4. Round this number to 0.67.
5. Move the decimal point 2 places to the right = 67.
6. Reduce the design 67%.

Now it is time to transfer the design from the page to the cloth.

MARKING TECHNIQUES FOR TRANSFERRING PATTERNS

There are many methods and products available to transfer designs from the page to the cloth. Building a repertoire of techniques will enable you to transfer designs regardless of the fabrics or construction methods used to create your quilt top. Every variable presents its own challenge. The more you know, the easier it will be to transfer designs onto light, dark, and printed fabrics and successfully stitch on patchwork and appliqué designs. *Heirloom Machine Quilting* by Harriet Hargrave and *Mastering Quilt Marking* by Pepper Cory are excellent books presenting valuable information and a large variety of methods for marking your quilt tops.

More than once, Sharon Norbutas—designated National Quilters Association Masterpiece Quilter, retired Home Economics instructor, and mentor—offered me this valuable advice: "There are ten ways to do everything, five of them work, three of them are good, and you pick one." Here are a few ways to try.

Markers.

There are many fabric markers available today. Test any marker you are considering to ensure that the lines can be removed before you mark your quilt top. "Try before you cry" is a good recommendation to follow. A note of caution: Be careful using water-soluble and air-soluble markers. Heat can permanently set the fugitive dye contained in these pens. Do not iron the fabric after using these pens, and do not store your quilt top in a hot environment. Even a warm kitten sleeping on a pile of patchwork can be a danger to tops marked with these pens. Some fabric dyes can change color when they react with the color in these pens. Also, humidity can make the lines disappear before the designs are completely quilted. You must be willing to thoroughly wash your quilt to remove any residual chemicals after using these markers. Despite all of these warnings, I often mark quilts I intend to machine quilt with blue, water-soluble felt-tip markers.

For dark fabrics, many white fabric markers are available. Roxanne's Quilter's Choice pencil and General Pencil Company's Charcoal White are two products I have used for years to mark quilting designs.

Tip

If you are considering quilting a vintage top, be aware that many antique fabrics will not tolerate needling and will break under the needle's force. Marking old fabric is always risky. Many antique fabrics, particularly those from the nineteenth century, will not tolerate wet-washing. Avoid using products containing modern chemicals or those requiring water to remove their markings. Fragile fabrics could be damaged beyond repair.

Tracing

Tracing a design onto your quilt top before it is layered is one of the simplest methods of marking. Copy your patterns onto paper, using a thin, black, permanent felt-tip marker. Make the lines heavy enough to be seen through the fabric. Use a fabric pencil or fabric marker of your choice to trace the pattern onto your quilt. Be careful not to draw the lines too darkly on the fabric, as this may be difficult to remove. This method can be executed more easily by using a lightbox.

Making a Template

Templates can be made from a variety of materials. Commercially made templates have slots identifying the exterior and interior lines of the design. Sheets of thin plastic make sturdy pattern shapes that will hold sharp, clean edges. Try tracing the quilting design onto clear or frosted plastic and cutting out the overall outline image. Smaller interior shapes can be created separately and added onto the top after the larger outline design is marked. This eliminates the tedious and often difficult task of cutting slots into plastic. Drawing around solid shapes is easier than penciling through channels.

Another material used for templates is lightweight cardboard. During the 1920s and 1930s many quiltmakers used cereal boxes. Glue a copy of the quilting motif onto thin cardboard and cut out the outline shape. Simple slots can be cut to add reference marks for drawing interior design lines. Worn-out cardboard templates served quilters well, generations ago.

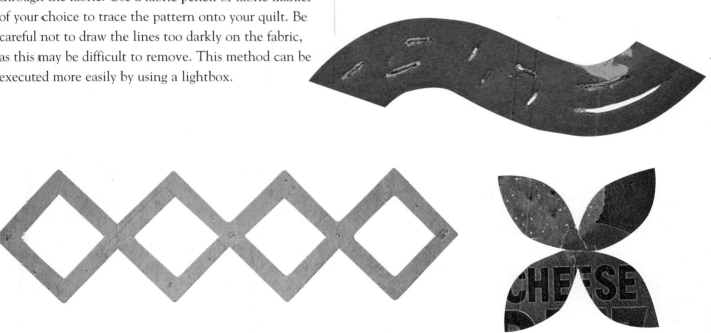

Grids

Use rulers of various widths not only to mark straight lines but to maintain a consistent distance between the lines. The 45°- and 60°-angle rulers help establish and retain diagonal grids. Throughout history, grids were stitched on many patchwork and appliqué quilts. Both the angles and the spacing between the lines could vary greatly, even on the same quilt. Hanging diamonds is an example of a grid design that can be casual and uneven, as on utilitarian quilts, or exact in its spacing.

Tip

Audition the angle, direction, and spacing of a grid by laying flat-sided wooden chopsticks on top of your piecework.

NO-MARK TECHNIQUES FOR TRANSFERRING PATTERNS

Perforated Paper Stencils

Machine quilters may want to try stitching through perforated paper stencils. Lightweight tear-away vellum paper will work, or try the tissue-like medical paper used for years to cover doctors' examining tables. Trace the design onto paper with a permanent marker or pencil, and layer up to eight additional sheets. Pinning or stapling the stack together keeps the papers from shifting. Using an unthreaded sewing machine equipped with a large needle, sew through all the layers, perforating the lines of the design. Remove each perforated copy and place it onto the quilt, ensuring that no safety pins will be obstructing the stitching sequence. Stitch directly through the paper. Gently tear the paper away, being careful not to disturb the stitches. Do not use the original tracing. Some markings may be trapped under the thread, and the design will be darker once stitched onto the quilt. Check with your sewing machine dealer if your machine will not operate without thread.

Sticky Stuff

Masking and painter's tape can help sustain an even grid. Self-adhesive shelf paper can be cut into silhouettes, and office-supply labels and decorative stickers are available in a variety of shapes and sizes. These can guide stitching in circles, squares, hearts, and more. Remember to test for any adhesive residue that might remain after the pattern is removed, and do not leave these sticky patterns in place for an extended length of time.

MAKE IT YOUR OWN

Please take liberties and be creative when designing patterns for your quilts. Use these printed designs as a guide. Try freehand drawing each image onto your quilt. The resulting variations will more closely represent the designs of quilts stitched generations ago, long before modern technology, laser-punched templates, and copy machines.

Bibliography

Beyer, Alice, *Quilting*. South Park Recreation Department, Chicago, 1934.

Brackman, Barbara, *Encyclopedia of Pieced Patterns*. Paducah, Kentucky: American Quilter's Society, 1993.

Fox, Sandi, *California Bound*. Los Angeles: FIDM Museum & Library, Inc. 2002.

Garoutte, Sally, ed., *Uncoverings*: 1980. ed. Laurel Horton and Sally Garoutte: 1989, Laurel Horton 1990, Kathlyn Sullivan: 2005 Mill Valley, California, 1980. San Francisco 1989–1990. Lincoln, Nebraska, 2005: American Quilt Study Group.

Godey, Louis, *Godey's Lady's Book*. Philadelphia, Pennsylvania: 1830–1836, 1859, 1860.

"Grandma" Dexter Quilting Designs. Elgin, Illinois: Virginia Snow Studios.

Grandmother's Perforated Quilting Patterns. St. Louis, Missouri: W.L.M. Clark, Inc.

Hinson, Dolores A., *Quilting Manual*. Hearthside Press, Inc. New York: 1966. Reprinted by Dover.

Kiracofe, Roderick, *The American Quilt*. New York: Clarkson Potter, 1993.

Lipset, Linda Otto, *Remember Me: Women & Their Friendship Quilts*. San Francisco: Quilt Digest Press, 1985.

Orlosky, Patsy and Myron, *Quilts in America*. New York, London, Paris: Abbeville Press, 1992.

The Priscilla Patchwork Book. The Woman's World Service Library, Manning Publication Company, Chicago: 1932.

Ver Mehren, Hubert and Mary, *Colonial Quilts* booklet. 1936.

Webster, Marie D., *Quilts: Their Story and How to Make Them*. Tudor Publishing Co., New York: 1915. Reprinted by Practical Patchwork, Santa Barbara, California, 1990.

Watts, Kristen, ed., *American Quilt Classics 1800–1980*. Charlotte, North Carolina, Mint Museum of Craft and Design, 2003.

Ladies' Art Company, *Quilt Pattern Book, Patchwork and Appliqué*. St. Louis, Missouri: 1922.

About the Author

Photo by Philip Kinney

JENNY CARR KINNEY has been making quilts since 1968 and professionally teaching quiltmaking for over 25 years. She taught clothing construction when she joined the fashion design program at Ventura College. In 1999, Jenny developed the quilting curriculum—offered as elective credits for students studying to obtain an associate's degree through the Home Economics Department. Currently Jenny teaches all sections of quilt construction, pattern drafting, instruction writing, and quilt history.

Jenny has appeared on Simply Quilts and teaches nationally. She specializes in historically inspired antique reproductions and period-appropriate quilting motifs sewn with modern equipment and using today's techniques.

She and her husband enjoy hot air ballooning and share their home with an inquisitive and now well-trained black Labrador retriever named Darby.

My darling dog, Darby, put his mark on the book … every shred of paper is Darby's doing. The repaired pages on the table are the work of my very good (and patient) friend Janis Farr. I'm so glad she likes puzzles. You can bet I won't leave anything lying around for Darby to edit again.

Photo by Jenny Carr Kinney

Photo by Jenny Carr Kinney

Great Titles *from*  C&T PUBLISHING

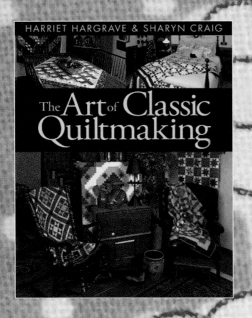

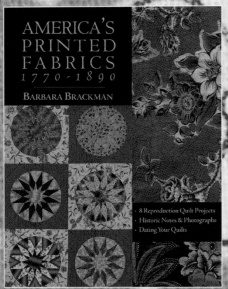